Machiavelli's Backyard

David Lohrey

SUDDEN DENOUEMENT
PUBLISHING

Published in 2017 by
Sudden Denouement Publishing
Houston, Texas
Website: www.suddendenouement.com
Email: suddendenouement@gmail.com

ISBN-13: 978-0999079607
ISBN-10: 0999079603

Cover Image – "Man, Tree Man, Wood, Bierke"
pixabay.com/en/man-tree-man-wood-bierke-artwork-2160602/

Acknowledgement

First and foremost, I want to thank Jasper who convinced me early on that he was a man of his word. This has meant a lot to me. How many times in one's life does one hear the word yes and know the other person means it? All of the writers at Sudden Denouement who dedicate themselves to the written word are an inspiration. My friends are so few and special: Bruce Feldman, Annette Aronowicz, Rickford Grant, and Ian Hunter have taken the trouble to read and comment on many of these poems. Richard Pell and Ellen Klyce have cheered me on. The acceptance of these poems for publication in various journals and magazines has been an enormous encouragement. I am especially thankful to Ellen Parker at *FRiGG*, *Otoliths'* Mark Young, Jay Dougherty at *Poetry Circle*, and *Sentinel Literary Journal's* Mandy Pannett. There are many others whose support has been much appreciated, but special thanks to Trevor Conway for featuring my work on his website.

This book is gratefully dedicated to my wife, Yuka. She reminds me every day of the importance of humor in poetry but especially of its importance in life.

Forward

Discovering great poetry, or a great poet, is an event, a happening. I would go as far to state it is a transcendent moment in the life of one consumed by a passion for the written word. I remember these moments, the way one would remember the death of a family member or a first kiss. I can count on one hand the times when I was left breathless by the inspired words of poets. Discovering the work of David Lohrey is a moment in which the world stopped, for a brief moment, his work restored my faith in humanity.

From "*61 Is Fine By Me*" to "*Tokyo Express*," David's poetry is a manifestation of an artist at the top of his craft. I am honored to be part of his journey and have come to understand Lohrey to be an individual who shares my conviction for literature and a poet whose time has come. Sudden Denouement is honored to have the opportunity to publish this amazing collection of poetry. The world needs the poetry of David Lohrey, now more than ever. Publishing his work is the culmination of two dreams, two passions that line up perfectly to present his book to the world. I am deeply grateful for the impact Lohrey has had on my life, and it is my hope others will discover the beauty of his work and find his book to be as much of a gift as I do. Thank you, David Lohrey.

Jasper Kerkau

Sudden Denouement Publishing

Contents

Beside the Red Barn

Beside the red barn
at an intersection
between today and tomorrow,

a man from Alabama plays the banjo on his knee;
he whistles Dixie and wears a Confederate cap
with shoes by Nike.

Roy Rogers, his uncle, stands stark naked on his bed
eating a Milky Way, with a red bow tied around his penis;
his second wife Maybelline won't quit laughing.

Daniel Boone and Davy Crocket embrace with affection.

The mayor of San Antonio cries quietly at attention.

It's Thursday afternoon at 3.

No Rest for the Wicked

It is not only work that is part of the punishment.
I am dying for a cup of coffee but only have instant.
Mother says the recipes cannot be found in a cookbook.
What gives country singers their radiant smiles?

I've put 3 calls into "We Care" but nobody answers.
It is not only work that is part of the punishment.
She made him hang up whenever I called him.
Why won't they pick up at the suicide hotline?

He was brain dead for weeks but his heart wouldn't stop
beating. Mother kept asking questions but didn't like his
answers. It is not only work that is part of the punishment.
Why do people cry when they listen to music?

I rushed in but father had died before I could reach him.
She thought I was a burglar and screamed for the day nurse.
What do the dramas on television teach us?
It is not only work that is part of the punishment.

His funeral was cancelled because the earth was still
frozen. His brother demanded two priests from the Catholic
archbishop. She preferred singers and dancers with
pompoms and sparklers. He was cremated and placed in an
urn from a Japanese toy store.

It is not only work that is part of the punishment.

Evolution of Grief

I am a beached wail,
a lonesome dove without wings,
a caged hamster who's gnawed away
its paw.

I haven't done anything for which
I can be blamed. I'm like an anorexic
who's trying to disappear. Fifty
more pounds and I won't be able to stand.

I'd do anything to avoid responsibility.
I'd even give up sex. Better to be
repellent than to risk rejection.
Better to withdraw than be ignored.

Get out before someone pulls the alarm,
like a hoodlum fleeing through
the kitchen to avoid a raid.
I'll have to learn to pee sitting down.

Better to starve than to be fulfilled.
When you get too small to be loved,
you can say you are a worm. You'll be
like a frog, too weak to croak.

A million years on, you'll develop
the ability to spit blood. Your glistening
flesh will be toxic. You will be left alone at last.
You will finally have the rock all to yourself.

61 Is Fine By Me

Is 61 old?
It is my birthday and I called my mother.
She said how are you? And was disappointed
When I replied just fine.
"Are you happy to be getting older?"

Happy?
Does one have a choice?
Is it getting older or getting younger?
If one is 60, one becomes 61 or 59?
No, it's 61 or dying.

Getting older is fine by me.
I'm happy with another day.
When you're 11, you can think getting older
Is not for me. I'll marry mommy and be young forever.

I'd prefer older and tomorrow to
Staying young today and tomorrow.
Getting older and older is fine by me.
The alternative is dying, not getting finer.

Black and Blue

First the sky, black or blue, depending on the time.
By day, Memphis blazes, 100 degrees in the shade; the sky,
robin blue.
At night, there are lightning bugs galore and stars, eerie,
dazzling and quiet, as from the Mississippi, slaves once
dragged bales across cobblestones.

Color of my eyes? My mother's?
It was morning glories we beheld, not roses. Roses
come in black, not in blue. I did see father many times
but I don't remember his eyes.

White and black photographs show us in our pajamas
with little bows and arrows scrawled across the tops.
Bugles and drums decorate our blue bottoms.
Snow cones at Tobey Park were that hue, too.

All gone now: how large the Pippin loomed over the police
academy. German shepherds lunged at padded arms as men
in black set fires with smoke as thick as cotton candy.
Heading back, we devoured ten cent burgers at Fred
Montesi's and pocketed Beatles cards at the Woolworths.

From 2 to 6, TV's Happy Hal hawked fantastic wigs to kids
Like me with giant waxen lips. Friday nights, close to
midnight, Boris Karloff, our best friend, dropped in for
chips and dip and stolen Tootsie Pops.

The Pink Palace was dad's fortress of art and power,
in costumes, he designed himself: a clown, some whimsy,
a melancholic smile, despair, or an oriental stare;
in make-up and girdles, a sword, a pistol, a tunic or robe,
tights and sandals, shaped from plastic or leather.

Father directed: *Give them some cleavage. Show 'em your tits.*

Dress rehearsal: *You'll eat it and like it.*
Get your ass over here, or no dinner for you.
Mrs. Rosenthal? She wants the part?
Goddamn it! Would somebody get her the fucking script?
The actors above; a black man below, bathing in the
basement ditch, a smelly remnant of Jake's endeavors.
Dad still at it: *Stop talking and bring me two aspirin.*

I read the reviews of the greatest show on earth.
The boosters took stock:
"It is a miracle, stupendous, a brilliant start."
The theatre was packed; no one could get in.
He was selling tickets, ten bucks a shot
to crawl through the attic, to stand at the back.

Not wanting to stay—please no longer. Not one more hour,
not another minute, not five measly seconds more.
My mother couldn't get out of town fast enough.
She tried to quit drinking, to stop punishing herself,
for allowing him to insist on yes, always to demand the
store.

That father could ruin a dinner for a lousy buck is true.
Kool-Aid or pudding? Take one or the other. He saved 50
cents at Morrison's and lost my love. The grand master had
little to give; it was all show but no tell. *I'll have another
martini.*

Don't disturb his rest, dear mother cried. *This is our house.*
Get out of here!
So I reached out my five-year-old hand and fled from
Tennessee.
Why are you calling now? How dare you ask for money!

It feels right that the old man is dead. His heart was black
and blue. He beat himself up and beat me, too.
When I think of Memphis I think of death, but not from
long ago and not from yellow fever.
Brother Martin was first to go and then Vernon Presley's
loving son.

This December, the trees in our yard will come down,
felled by an ice storm, torrential and freezing. Birds will be
heard, not chirping but mocking.
Dad's gone now, thank goodness; there's only mother left.
The dogwoods stand silent, as her eyes watch, laughing.
There's much comfort knowing how much she loves the
bluff.

Bride of the Sky

It was her nose that caught my attention,
but not as a prim thing with a small IQ to match.
It was something grand like a tropical toucan.
As the poet's jar engulfed by rugged Tennessee,
this nose was more a presence than an object.
Her green eyes though were not jungle wild;
they took me to places like the Warsaw ghetto.
I think today of her as a thing of art, because like a carving
or, even more, an engraving, her features seem immortal.

We met in Paolo's car on the way to *Rio*, a local favorite.
She sat in front and I right in back behind her.
I had already met her nose.
I couldn't help myself and reached up to touch the nape
of her neck as a way to say hello. When we stopped
and got out of the car, she approached and whispered,
"I like the hand on the neck."

What a thing. The only time in my life I have loved
someone's nose. We fucked all the time, but she
didn't want anyone to know. I was only 23,
but felt freed from the unknown. Had it been another time
and place, we might have had a go, but we let things
flounder and blew the chance of a lifetime.

Marian had had giant soft tits and that is all there is to it.
She wondered aloud if that was what had drawn me, as they
had attracted others; she recited men's comments.
I'm sorry, my love, it isn't your chest, Not even
your beautiful green eyes. It is that majestic nose,
the beak of an eagle, the bride of the sky that did it.

Picasso had almost got her right with
his cave-dwelling ladies. She had the same angular

breasts and a grand Baroque ass.
She was cross-eyed, too, and carried that nose
with its high-arched bone. What he got wrong were the
feet, which were not like the Spaniard's lumbering ladies,
gigantic, but small. He hadn't caught her skin color either,
which was pale and creamy, not gray, coffee or gravy, nor
that most modern of hues, blue.

She'd had a searching mind, a sly smile,
a wicked, charming laugh – almost a cackle.
She was a little crazy. She used to bang
her head against the wall, and, she said,
Did it because she felt worthless. She could be
cold and hyper-critical, snobby and dismissive.
She was capable of violence. She once punched me in the
stomach and made me double over.

We lost touch. I saw her, though, sometime later.
She was down fifty pounds. She kept her nose and her
sexy laugh, but her thighs and marvelous ass were gone.
No longer ancient, she had become modern.
She was sleek and sickly like T.S. Eliot.
She was a ghost. She'd once, this Marian Striver, had
Eliot's appetite for things; now she bore his sorrows.

She still had her nose but had dropped her beguiling smile.
I knew then and there that something was irretrievably lost.
She was thin and less than lively. She was no longer
Rubens'; she belonged to Modigliani.
She was brittle and, I could see a mile away,
No longer interested in me. I went to our friend from São
Luís, who shrugged: "Some toucan prefer Venezuela."

Drink the Ramen

It rains every day but there is no water.

In Chitose-Funabashi, the puddles are fine and the river
runs wide,
But showers are on timers.

Take the wrappers off the bottles, keep the lettuce in the
larder,
The neighbors eye our bin.

This summer, lightning strikes harder but the rains lose
heart.
Locals don't taste the noodles, the flavor's in the broth.

It rains every day but there is no water.

Kiss of Life

Lips to cheek, the young father
sits wetting the baby's face
with his love. He leans into the child
who sits on his lap and smiles.
His nose grazes her chin.
He dazzles her with his grin.
She burbles back in enthusiasm.
He hangs his lip on her nose.
He kisses her and says hello, hello.
Daddy's love. Mommy's, too. She leans
over for a quick lick to establish contact.
They shoot me a glance and are proud.
They bring cheer to my scowl.

Baby time. Even Arabs believe in Father Christmas.
A father's love is not religious. We plant kisses
like Johnny Appleseed. We collect them like pollen.
Kisses turn fathers into bees.
The constant kiss, the planted lips.
The extended lip, the smooch:
lips rub lips and with that everything
is explained. This father's lips remain
extended like a monkey's eating lice.
Only here father is not ingesting, he is feeding,
dispensing medicine to his daughter
to ensure her happiness; magic,
to increase her sense of well-being.
It will be a long flight. Father never once withdraws.
They stay together, connected, and will remain so,
forever.

The Rottweiler Next Door

The Rottweiler next door killed my wife's pink
   Chihuahua, but spat out one ear.
We planted its ear in our flower bed next to
   the foxgloves under 3 inches of mulch.
It germinated, sending up coiled fronds 14" high.
   At the first rain, it died, the entire spectacle.

It barks at night, or so my wife says. She hears it.
   Lorraine, our Mexican maid from Oaxaca,
hears it, too. Her mole won first prize at the Pomona Fair,
   taking 1st place for color but 3rd for taste. It was the
color of blood that's been left out in the sun.

Lorraine calls everyone amigo except me. It's clear we are
   not friends, so she calls me mister or maestro.
She asks me every morning if I'd like some mud. Her ass
   is wider than our Maytag. She doesn't use pot
holders when she removes hot skillets from the stove.

The Rottweiler next door killed my appetite for life. It's a
   special breed bred for violence. He ate our pooch
whole, clamping down on its head and swallowing, as a
   snake devours a mouse. Only Judy Collins can
mend my heart. Only the past offers escape. From here on
   out all our neighbors are Rottweilers.

For the Coal Miners

Ok, ok, already. Nat King Cole,
Billy Holiday, Mona Lisa: take everything
away I love, but do not remove the
coal miners.

It'd be like banning garbage collection.
It's too much change. Go ahead: end NASA.
Bring the astronauts back, but don't force
the miners to come up for air.

We need them right where they are.
Let them stay underground. It makes
us feel better. They give us liberty; their
presence down there makes being here better.

There's a lot more to it than rocks, Mr. President.
The people will do just fine without men and women
in orbit, but we can't live without knowing
men are digging beneath the surface.

Just ask D.H. Lawrence. Could you live another minute
without "Sons and Lovers"? His father was a miner and his
mother, a school teacher. Have you heard that somewhere
before? It's mythological. It's Adam and Eve, I'm telling
you.

If heterosexuality means anything, the answer is to be
found in the coal miner and his future widow. Beauty and
the beast. It's the architecture of hope and despair.
Do you think the Chinese will ever stop digging?

If we stop now, we'll never get to the center of the earth.
Have you ever met a miner who wasn't a poet?
If we close the mines, we'll kill country music. We'll make

Johnny Cash obsolete. Dolly Parton will die.

It'd be like having dinner without Coca-Cola. Well… I could do without the soda, but not without the miners. There's no English literature without coal miners. We are a luck society, and where else to learn of luck if not from a coal miner?

There isn't a day goes by without miners somewhere being buried in rubble. Their widows function as modern society's last Greek chorus. Without them, we are on our own. Our tragedy would become forgotten melodrama.

From The Bird's Nest

From The Bird's Nest

high above
swaying in the wind,

four baby crows
fell to the patio below
and landed intact and quite alive;

a man came out to look
at his little neighbors
who had just dropped in.

The great black mother
circled above
keeping her thoughts
to herself, then
screeched to warn her

chicks who
peeped and hopped
about,

until one by one they fell to their side
and abruptly died,

stiff and silent in still air.

Hand to Mouth

We die alone because old people stop fucking.
Once you give up sex, you're on your own.
That so-called friend, your partner, no longer
returns your phone calls.
She's found someone, as people used to say.

She's found somebody else is a polite
way to say she's no longer fucking you.
Dating is not about popcorn.
More than friends is the opposite of only.

Who controls the hands, controls the sex.
Your life is in her hands.
Hold them (down), tie them (up), or cuff them:
there is no on the other hand.
Her hands are all over the place.

What he needs is a hand job.
But you can hold his hand instead.
Go ahead, if it's clean.
Isn't that what "give your hand in marriage"
means?

Stolen kisses.
He had a hand in it. He conned her out of it.
The crime of the century was an act of indiscretion.
He pinched her bottom but she didn't flinch.
Give an inch and he'll take a mile.

Copulation won't prevent death.
I never said that.
It's Philip Roth's brutal insight I have in mind:
Without sex other people don't matter.
Without sex, there'd be nothing but hand to hand combat.

Humpty Dumpty

The young, rich and poor, think
Nintendo is superior to the Sistine Chapel.
They admire Steve Jobs more than Michelangelo.
If not that, then they are judged equally as artists,
as creative forces. People's idea of culture consists of
computer games and videos. In China, the favorite film of
the 15 to 20 crowd is *Roman Holiday* with Audrey
Hepburn. In America, the young esteem *Rogue Nation* and
Harry Potter as works of cinematic art, and not a soul says
otherwise. The kids here watch porno in college and want
to get rich. From their point of view, there isn't anything of
value that isn't on Google or YouTube. Their answer to art
is to take a dick pic or a selfie with their mouths full of
cherries.

Given the choice, which would you prefer,
a can of chicken noodle or a painting of Campbell Soup?
Pop art drives people from the museums. Pop music
hasn't helped either. Who wants to go to the symphony
to listen to *Pop Goes the Weasel*? At a basic level,
people get tired of calling dreck, art. *Star Wars* killed film
going. The cartoonists have taken over; the banks own the
studios. People demand shag carpeting in their houses,
but they don't want pictures of it on their walls.
It's the feel that helps people relax, not the image.
That's where pop art gets it wrong.

There can be no art without skill. Without training and
powers of endurance, nobody can learn to throw a pot. The
kids can bang a drum or bang each other, but the oboe takes
years of practice, as does the piccolo. We promote
creativity but not obedience. There is no discipline except

on the football field where the coaches kick the idiots off the team. The so-called artists are praised to the sky even when they skip rehearsal. Fat girls fight to join the ballet. Kids without lips want to play trumpet. Something has to give. Someone has to say no. We do need creativity but we also need tyrants. Monster geniuses who have no patience. Prima donnas, tantrum throwers - not sensitivity trainers - are what's needed. Bring back the Gods. Otherwise, the arts will vanish and in their place we'll have docile people, like the Swiss, who after hundreds of years of contentment invented clocks with punctual cocks that sing.

Landscape with Lemonade Stand

Would you turn your back on the sun
for a ham or tuna sandwich?
You might say no, but I don't believe you.
We are not lovers of the sun, modern man.
The sun is no longer something noble;
tt is nothing more than Earth's heater.

Would you prefer some apricot juice in a glass,
or one last glance at the setting sun?
Something to cool you, or a last-minute look
at the planet's source of light?
You'd take the glass, even if there were sand in it.

Would you strap wings to your back and head out
for the nearest star?
Icarus was a damned idiot and you know it.
He is seen as a fool, not a saint or a hero.
We moderns get the message loud and clear;
His death is seen as a clear warning, not a thrill.

Wouldn't you rather live in a cave than be left to wing it?
We moderns know a thing or two, just ask Picasso.
There's a reason he painted men and women with clay feet.
We are lumbering cave men carrying clubs, not birds of
flight. Our instinct is to head for the fire and defend it,
not to fly away in search of hope.

Would you pass up success for eternal bliss or honor?
Where I come from such talk sounds ridiculous, even
corny. There's a reason our Founding Fathers favored the
Romans. The Greeks were too willing to throw it all away
for glory. We have to hold on to what's on offer. We
moderns know not to head for the sun but to line up at the
counter.

Triumph of the Will

Our President makes a point of greeting little old ladies
in the White House. He makes a grand entrance and hugs
them. His wife does a jig. I've seen them.
He gives them a medal and congratulates them
on reaching the ripe old age of 100. Astronauts, soldiers,
artists and old women: who could blame him?

Among the many accomplishments, aging is one of them.
Survival deserves attention. Steven Sondheim even wrote a
song about it, "I'm still here."

But I wonder.

Does the President greet them in his impeccable French?
Does he ask them if they know their lieder? Do they
discuss Greek declensions, debate the proper use of verb
cases? Teddy Roosevelt once did, before dying in his sleep
five days into the New Year in 1919.

Our leaders and their earnest followers no longer value
education. They can speak but that's about it. Few
Americans can balance a check book.
Many can barely read and write. I'm talking about those
born in the USA. They eschew 19th century education.
They've dropped the classics. They don't want Latin.

Instead, they're praised for surviving like raccoons and
mealy bugs. The hive lives. Put your ear to the wall. It's
hot. The bees create heat. And then they drop.
The ants eat their dead bodies.
The President stands ready to pin a medal on the little old
lady's bosom and says, "Bravo. You did it," as though
she'd just returned from the North Pole.

Paradise Is Demanding

It must be thrilling to know everything.
Girls used to be so full of doubt but now they say,
Sure I'm sure. I say 1970, she says Nixon bombed
Cambodia. When I was a kid I found a brontosaurus under
my corn flakes. Today I get all of world history at the end
of my tootsie pop.

The bodies, you cry. The dead bodies in the lobby.
Why can't I reply, my mother's violets in the window box
Remind me of tiny flamethrowers. The poor don't need
money. It's the rich who are always short.

Everywhere I go, I'm an unknown quantity.
Why do you invade my territory? They bring me hot dogs
when I order origami. In China they begged me to stay, but
here, why won't you go?

Don't ask, how are you? It's an intimate question.
I think it is privacy and so do you, but here it's a matter of
public policy. Infants wear reading glasses to mommy and
baby English classes. You are in another country

When students dance into class wearing chiffon tutus.
They hide their hair in green. One student's yellow toenails
match his glasses; another's braces are as sparkling as her
tiara.

On trains, the girls don't keep their legs together. One sees
Bandaged knees and little hands spreading skin cream.
The Santa Barbara coffee shop in Roppongi brews no
coffee; it serves poached eggs on a bed of lettuce.

Paradise is demanding.
The bodies pile up to my Adam's apple.

My daughter's into cranes and pandas.
Are we punished for ignoring corpses?

Must I feed the neighbors, take care of tornadoes,
split the atom, and make ice cubes?
I can barely add 2+2. I can't remember to change my socks.
Last week I lost the Empire State Building.

I want my teddy bear.
Can't I like pandas, too?
Thou shalt not kill.
Is that not enough for you?

The busker asks for what's left over.
Must I share?
I have lots to spare but none for you.
Why can't I say that?

Muddy Water

Mississippi is America without the lying.
My granddaddy used to say that. It's not just
another state across the state line, he'd say.
That's the State of Mississippi. They want
you to believe it is the state of refinement.

Not that there's anything wrong with fine dining.
Grandfather could send you to a nice place in Clarksdale,
Vicksburg, or even Tupelo. But he couldn't recommend
baseball on Sunday, not in the State of Mississippi.

The Eudora Welty Society doesn't want to accept it.
They say it is all about gracious living, Southern-style.
If you ask the Friends of Walker Percy, the kind of men
who use their wives' hairspray, they'd explain that there are
no toilets in Mississippi, just rooms for gentlemen and
powder.

They just love poetry readings and recitations.
Conferences on flower arranging and ophthalmology.
The folks in Oxford are especially fond of the Japanese
tea ceremony. Pissarro and the French Impressionists
are a big draw at the local art gallery.

University life as we all know concentrates on smart
dialogue. Discussions and lectures dominate the schedules
of busy young people preparing for a future of three-
bedroom mortgages. At half-time, on days of play, the
young ladies strut their wares. They only carry
pom-poms to hide their daggers.

Mississippi is a tougher place than people want to admit.
Good girls only give head when the home team wins. Nice
people are appalled by the Negroes. Chains down there

weren't used to keep black folks from running; they were used to beat them to death.

Grandfather didn't want to die for pecan pie
as other folks did, and not for anything else for that matter.
Not the gooseberry wine, the catfish, the hushpuppies, or
the grits; not for nothing, as they used to say. Not even for
the fried pickles white folks always say are good enough to
die for.

Not for granddaddy. He wasn't about to get himself killed
over some salad with earl and vinegar, and certainly not
over some shit talk at the barrel of a shotgun. See, back in
1966, and not that far from the highway of that name, my
granddaddy Minnis and his team from Wilson, Arkansas
won the biggest ballgame of the season.

They were so famous, a radio station announcer challenged
their team to head over for a fight to the finish, a
Mississippi Delta Championship. The boys climbed into a
big yellow school bus, crossed the mighty river, and headed
south on I-55 from Downtown Memphis.

They were greeted upon arrival by the local sheriff
and his cow-shit-stained deputies who aimed their shotguns
at their heads and shouted, "Niggers don't play ball down
here, So ya'll better git back yonder."

Granddaddy Minnis and his buddies headed back home.
They didn't talk that night of word choice or syntax.
Walker Percy and Eudora Welty never came up. Not them
and not Grisham and not Faulkner neither. They talked that
night of how dangerous it was down in Mississippi
and swore to God not to go back again.

Eat a Peach

The prostate goes.
The plumbing breaks.
The penis drips.
It isn't pretty.
Sagging boobs are the least of it.

Being young sucks but for other reasons.
The balding head started balding years ago.
I was prepared for it.
But not for this.

I'll never pat an ass again.
I want to touch and be touched,
But let's face it: I'm too old and stinky.
I used to count on that chance to get closer.
What's missed is not the fornication but the flirting.

Bodily secretions, special strains of sweat,
Rare sovereign odors once confined to my nether regions.
Little spills don't add up to much,
But the constant throat clearing, sneezing, and nose
dripping?
Death is close. I can taste it.

The final feet, the final door:
I'm working my way towards the finish.
Sometimes I still look for encouragement.
But the only sign I have is one tiny hair on my nose.
Perhaps tomorrow I'll have two.

Nightly News

"I have no friends, and you are one of them."
This tastes exactly like chocolate mousse.
I have so many friends who mean nothing to me.

The last friend I ever had greeted my every word with joy.
She had much to live for but seemed alive for me.
Others treat friendship as a burden.

They ignore me and it makes them feel guilty. Every
greeting stings like a Chinese water torture. Drip. The only
aspect of our friendship remaining is the hope of its finally
ending. Drop.

I've been waiting for a reply. Left several messages.
It's been two weeks now without an answer. I've been
consumed by this topic. I've been eager for discussion.

"What does that have to do with me?" Drip.
My good friend replies to my news of the lacrosse team at
Duke falsely accused of rape. That's one way to end a
friendship. Drop.

People start reading different papers. Justice becomes
another hobby. It's not that love disappears, or not only; it's
an absence of interest, an indifference. "Warm regards"
won't do it.

Old friends cease to exist. The friendship ends,
like one's faith in God. You can't save a friendship;
you must save yourself.

The Jungle Beneath

Say what you will, the Amazon is not the Mississippi.
It may be long and merry, but it is not muddy or murky.
It's sleek and shiny like a child's string of licorice, a blend
of Whiskey and coffee. The Amazon runs black, not
brackish, but laps beneath the cashew groves in a hue,
something like copper.

Piranha, remember, are carnivores, like hyena and humans.
They swim in schools crowding and jostling like kids at
dismissal. They assemble just beneath the surface which
looks as flat as a classroom blackboard. They don't hunt
alone as sharks do, circling for attack; the school moves as
one.

They crowd the depths, massed and swarming, hysterically,
like disturbed bees. The same as little boys, they can't stand
to be left behind. Once they smell blood, they make their
move, attacking as a gang of teenage thugs, delivering
blows and landing sucker punches. They run in vicious
packs like their cousins in the forest, wolves.

It's a cowardly wish that prefers to cut and run. It's a
reluctance to take responsibility. The key is not to go in for
the kill but to strip the naked carcass to the bone. Into this
ravenous mass the fisherman lowers his baited hook like a
teacher's stick of chalk. His line descends into the watery
darkness black as ink, weighted with chunks of raw red
meat.

The fisherman drops his line, like a miner down the shaft.
The water's color is sinister. To fall in would be like diving
into an open grave, not drowning but disappearing. The
river water runs like mascara. One waits and waits as on a
country road at midnight. If lucky, a toucan will fly by,

delivering a rainbow; otherwise, it promises to be a dark day.

Once caught, the little monsters with jaws like bear traps are scaled and gutted, then grilled on an open fire. One is ecstatic with one's catch, grateful to have made it. Being attacked and eaten by piranha would resemble an elegant giraffe brought down and picked apart, except that giraffe seem so calm and still when being devoured, while humans tend to flail.

Sociology 101

Not oily, not greasy: creamy.
That's it. Liberals are creamy.
The New Yorker is creamy.
What else? Business Class.
Who? Obama.
Clinton? No. Slick.
Tanya Harding? Al Sharpton?
What else is creamy? Hollywood, north of Sunset.
No, not Hollywood. Beverly Hills. Now, that's creamy!
Get it? Pico Boulevard is greasy.
Tom Hanks is creamy.
Seinfeld. Ellen. Definitely Oprah.

You see what I am saying?

It works. Divide the world
And it all makes sense.
The affluent prefer creamy.

New car salesmen are creamy.
Used: oily or greasy, depending on the model.
Used foreign car salesmen are definitely greasy.
Check out a ten-year-old Mercedes.

It works.

Department store clerks used to be creamy.
Now it's all self-service, so who knows?
The Kennedys: 50/50.
JFK? Creamy. Robert? Hard to say.
No one's creamy at Walmart.
Target's the same. There's
Nothing creamy about McDonald's,
Except in Japan and Hong Kong.

Everything is creamy at the ballet.
I'm telling you, it's foolproof.
Bill Gates is creamy. Steve Jobs, silken.

How about Trump? What about the new President?
His daughter Ivanka is creamy.
He's another matter.
Gold plating is not creamy.

It's sleazy.

Kabuki Café

The chef stirs the pancake mix
and stirs me, too. I love her
masculine bowtie. She looks like
a soda fountain clerk circa 1959.

She keeps her hair cut smart
and wears slacks. She has
a flat chest and works at a brisk pace.
If she were a boy she'd make
me laugh. As it is, she makes me swoon.

It's not that I'm into ogling chicks.
Good lord, no. I just appreciate
the effort, the development of
a caring soul who knows how
to use a whisk. She doesn't
just throw things together. She's
not just killing time.

Efficiency and excellence are
so rarely found. It's a thrill
to see a girl embody both.
The Japanese understand these things.
It's not just the sushi; it's in
the way they bend. You find it
in their insincerity. It's a performance.
They're like ballerinas on the stage, not idle
dancers in their dressing rooms.

It is indeed like kabuki. Their actions
mask their pain. They study movement;
they rehearse each step. They want to know
who you are before saying hello. Otherwise,
they don't know what to say. In a land

where speaking out of turn could get you killed,
they don't waste words.

Visitors get the cold shoulder
because they have not been introduced.
We're like the help at a wedding
in the Hamptons, told to serve
the champagne and not to speak. Invisibility
is not due to race, it's because we lack
consequence. In the West, a greeting
could lead to marriage. Here, hello goes
nowhere. It's better to greet strangers
with silence.

It is cruel. Many can't see it. Some can't
take it. Travelers temple-hop from Akasaka
to Kyoto in the belief they are welcome.
That's one way of looking at it.
What's more likely is that the orgasm and the ready
smile are put on for your pleasure. Each and every minute
is an agonized display. Secretly, the Japanese
can't wait for you to return home. They can't wait
for the curtain.

Stop the Forest Fires

I have a mind to cut your neck.

There are no apples in this poem;
not a lot of mist either,
save for the spray of blood
that decorates the corridor
from the slit in your fatty flesh.

There's an ugly image for you.
I'd call that gratuitous
violence; far more so than
blowing someone's head off.
Cutting flesh is surely harder
than setting fire to a charger.

Kaboom! Ratatattat. Those
sounds belong to a different era:
no doubt sounds familiar to Al Capone,
when killing was done neatly,
corpses were left to rot intact.
Now killers eat their victims,
not only burying their enemies in the ground,
but climbing down in there with them.

We've become violent.
Everyone tries his best to be
kinder but decides meaner is wiser.
Being nice won't get you far;
pursing one's lips won't get you past the bouncer
and without that, you can't get inside.
Better learn to kill.

Lady Gaga (I saw her) praised
Hillary for being made of steel,
a tough broad she is, ready for anything.

That got my attention. I thought, wow!,
she's even better than Marie Antoinette;
she's offering fans two slices of cake, not one.

But the violence stays because it's fun.
If you can't bring yourself to do the deed yourself,
at least you can watch.
Americans love a close-up;
it's the only way to see death.
Let's look together.

Meanwhile, the apple tree is hibernating.
The little bears are sleeping through this season.
They're waiting for the killing to stop.
Their eyes are misty; they're tearing up, in point of fact.
It's not easy seeing your mother skinned alive.
Where are the park rangers?

Holy Smoke I.
Tenancy

I've seen a lot of churches. That lovely
Greek Orthodox on New York's Upper West Side,
its interior powder blue and white. Oh, wow.
And in Rome, my God, the Santa Maria della Vittoria,
and on any street in San Miguel de Allende,
or take Landau Island between Macau and Hong Kong;
churches are everywhere but not here.

They've been abandoned like sharecropper shacks
not long ago on the way to Little Rock or in Mississippi.
The wind blows through them, they're used in desperation,
to protect one from the weather, for crude copulations,
or for defecating in the cold. They come in handy.

To get protection from the cold, some privacy
for a long-postponed urination. Is that all churches
are good for? Water closets for the poor? Such folly,
such desperation; was it once called desiccation?
Warring factions such as believers and non-believers
share a bathroom. Blasphemy is lonely.

Holy Smoke II.
Depths of Disaffection

Are churches meant as cold storage?
Nothing more than closets for Christian artifacts,
bins for Renaissance rubbish?
A filing cabinet for foolishness,
a site for buried knights,
retarded kings and perverse priests,
with postcards: two for a dollar.

What an end to human charity.

To be closed off and boarded up like an old
vaudeville house, like theatres on the Keith/Albee circuit,
silent movie houses of the soul,
demonstrations of human folly
and a little devil worship, like LA's Ambassador Hotel,
where Robert Kennedy bled to death,
right next to the Coconut Grove.

Nothing more than mommie dearest,
episodes of human anguish, dramatizations
of belief and superstition; a house full of Halloween
masks, a closet of soiled kimono,
a toilet with no plumbing.

Holy Smoke III.
Indifference

The gargoyles are watching.
Those naughty faces stare from the belfry.
They stick their stone tongues out and wave their pricks
at those passing below. Some are pissing
on those who shuffle along the pavement.

They rain greetings on passers-by,
cursing at their indifference.
Look up and you'll see the faces
of the angels and the devils;
Their grimaces and tight smiles greet you.
Go in or cross the street, quickly.
Get out of the way of the golden showers.

Why else place monsters on God's sacred palace?
Scowling goblins, volcanic midgets, smug angels
growl or grimace and spit right in their faces,
reminding those on their way their path is blocked.
They'll never get away. The end awaits.
Death is true. Look forward to it,
face it, or live out one's lousy life in despair.

Holy Smoke IV.
Murder in the Cathedral

Those Baroque cherubs with bare asses cling
to the cathedral's ceiling, plucking golden harps,
as they tug at human hearts.
They hang like bats from the ceiling, chubby tots,
babies, not even toddlers. Gazing down,
they denounce vanity but celebrate the divine.

In the courtyard lies the monastery's beer hall,
a haven for families and alcoholics.
The once sacred place has been turned into an attraction;
St. Jerome as another Mickey Mouse, a sacred Donald
Duck. The gargoyles are mere decorations,
There for our amusement, there as ghouls
and goblins meant to rile or to tickle.

Did the Soviets have it right?
Kill off the Christians and rebuild the churches.
Bring in the tourists! Against all warnings,
written and spoken, tourists snap selfies, dick pics in the
pews. Husband climbs the ladder while wife plays look-out.
To break off the cherub's tiny prick. That's where we're at.
Next she'll ask the priest for his autograph.

If such sights were never meant to be uplifting
but only for distracting or merely for haunting,
meant not to preoccupy, not to impart wisdom,
but only to amuse, like taking in a motion picture,
riding a roller coaster or visiting a brothel,
then churches were built for fools.

They've become destinations like park benches and
peaches, like restaurants with patios. The priest sucks
strawberries and cruises cute waiters. He orders the tilapia

with a side of organic honey. Who is he kidding?
No wonder we imagine priests, like everyone else, with
hard-ons. Who ever thought priests not strong enough to
resist what all men know is sordid? Masterbation, say what
you will, is not a celebration; whatever the elaboration, it is
never more than a consolation. But without belief, how can
one be expected to see a priest as any different?

Barnum & Bailey Chaos

There is nothing sadder than an old elephant at the zoo.
All alone, the color of tarmac; a gigantic mouse behind
bars. She stands at the ready, to turn around and around. By
the end of the day, she'll be fit for a shower and a long cry.
What's an elephant to do, chained to the ground, with a 6-
year child the only one who understands her pain?

I say, throw a peanut at her head. Pick up a chunk of rock.
Hop on its back and stick its ear. That'll teach it to dance.
Shout, "Go!" Hit it over and over again, the way you do
your wife and kids. When you're through with the elephant,
you can move on more important things, like burning
churches and killing doctors. Take it out on them, too. Why
stop with the dumb elephant and your shitty family? You
too can be effective, get yourself all worked up if you are
of the mind, pour gasoline all over and set yourself on fire.

When we kill elephants, we kill ourselves. These killing
sprees are assassinations. Don't kid yourself. It's murder.
Whoever said so, and it's probably your daughter, is right.
The decimation of the elephants, and that goes for gorillas
and anteaters, too, is self-destructive. It's annihilation of
the soul. It's a catastrophe of thought. Pure Neanderthal, a
spasm of base instinct. But then so is the murder of man.
Keep in mind, it is happening every day of the week and it
is not because they are poor.

He murdered his sister because he has no money is a
sinister joke told by the devil. Our heads need to be
examined. Here, it's becoming a killing field
like Rwanda or Cambodia before it. Incredibly,
decent people are confused; they are not sure it's wrong.
One thing for sure, it's a lot of fun. Put a cap in his ass.
HAHAHAHA.

Now that we've stripped our youth of their humanity,
what's next? I'll tell you what's coming: mass killings.
Human life is worth nothing in a place like this.
You might as well drive the herd over a cliff.

Domestic Violence

What an end. She's stopped talking.
She's no longer responding.
I don't understand. I want
to be understanding.

Be polite, I say, keep quiet.
Pretend nothing's happened.
Don't make an ass of yourself.
Pretend to be an English gentleman.

But it's odd to be dropped,
I've got to admit, or am I being shunned?
No discussion, no explaining.
Just a forceful ending, entirely one-sided.

Shunning is stunning; it's an aggressive act,
an assertion. An imposition, a commanding position.
"Just shut up and go."
Say good-bye and don't look back.

I feel the boot on my neck.
Thank you. It's harsh but direct.
She steps harder and shouts, "Shut up.
You're as good as dead."

Shunning is an act of cunning.
It's brutal and, above all, cold. Get up
and go, without a word. What a send-off.
It's a lot tougher than "fuck off."

But there was something there.
We'd been friends, not lovers. Not strangers.
Not neighbors. 40 years. I could have spoken at the
podium, teaching good relations. I loved her.

Not so fast. It was never so, she says.
That's a misinterpretation; it's not true.
Her foot comes down again on my neck and presses harder.
It's a figment of your imagination.

I must have done something,
Something very wrong to be ignored. I
said something or did something, I'm not sure.
Wouldn't you want to talk it over?

Shunning is not withdrawing.
It is not an act of defense.
It is an attack. It is offensive.
She expects me to disappear.

But we were friends, there had been kisses.
Like sister and brother, united and connected.
I knew her parents, knew her brother.
Her mother was once my best friend.

She was once gracious, thoughtful and attentive.
This harshness is quite new. Now she's very rigid,
even frigid. This assertion of power seems suddenly tonic:
bracing, pompous, even gleeful. It's a betrayal.

What a cunt. This is no friend of mine.
I'd never cut her off just like that.
Her mother wouldn't have allowed it.
There is an idea behind this act,
perhaps another person, a manipulation.

Must I now be turned into a stranger?
Is there another at work in this effort?
Has she been seduced by some diabolical fool?
I've got to get to the bottom of this.

Our friendship was tied to another.
There was little else holding us together.
We came to each other through her mother. My God!
I think I understand what may have happened.

Now that her mother's dead, daughter desires
to see the end. She'd done. She wants closure.
I've been nothing but demanding.
She has in so many ways been obliging.
She must have wondered when it would stop.

It's a miracle she was as helpful as she has been.
I regret not showing better judgment.
It's best to go quietly. We'll clear the air in the future.

It has been a pleasure knowing her.
I respect her desire to cease communication.

I won't write again.

Death Is Not a 5-Star Hotel

That was it. I wasn't able to be free,
wasn't prepared to carry the load, not entirely.
I was too young. And nobody took up the slack.
Absolutely not, so I drifted away. I paddled away,
down to a less vibrant part of the river and dropped
my line where there were no fish.

This can happen. One is left to fish without bait.
The water is torn by passing boats. The noise scares
some, but not the piranha. They're not so easily
fooled. They take the bait but not the hook. They bite with
care. They eat around the hook. And you wait in the black
water all day or for years, hoping for a break. You sit in a
boat that's not moving. You sit in the shade with the jungle
behind you.

You watch the toucan flying above. You whistle.
You wave and the people wave back. "I have friends."
You wait. You watch. You look. You listen, with the
piranha churning beneath you. The water is not green or
brown like mud. The water is black like a samurai's
topknot or a hearse at an Italian funeral. It reminds me of
the entrance to the Baglioni in Rome, only you won't find
a hotel like that where I am.

One learns to survive. The tiny flesh-eaters feast without
anger. Their desperation is instinctive. Their motivation is
survival. One is taught to prepare. My guide reminds me to
stay alert. Hemingway wanted to get things right. He had
an obsession with accurate observation. The imagination
can create distractions. He preferred despair to fantasy.
So did J.P. Morgan.

I am floating on water that is still. The sun doesn't have much longer. There are no stars in the sky, no moon in the river. The water is black like an open grave. I can imagine the fury beneath. I can feel their anticipation. It reminds me of Rothko's Chapel. It has no flowers. My guide laughs. We haven't had a bite. We should have made a move. Now it's too late. Even the toucan have stopped flying.

A Charlie Brown Christmas

Could there be anything worse?
Linus plays well but it's too slow.
The air, thick with smoke, stinks.
Nostalgia is philosophy without hope.

Christmas with cartoon characters
is like a funeral with mannequins.
Looking back isn't anything more
than an admission of guilt.

Mos Def would know what to do.
If you add motherfucker to every hallelujah
the patrons cheer up. We miss the past
because we're not good enough, not for yesterday,
never mind last week.

We're like high school drop-outs
returning for graduation, there to
watch our friends take a giant step.
We're a nation on the sidelines,
gentiles at a bar mitzvah.

We haven't done our homework;
we never study. We're going through the motions,
attending class but not arriving prepared.
We left our books in the locker. Sorry.

The losers have been getting prizes.
The experiment is over. Limos
at 6th grade graduation count for nothing.
The hundred dollar bill divided by one thousand
doesn't cut it.

Some are convinced we're on a winning streak,

but we missed the start. Now we're talking
with our lawyers about a second chance.
But the winner's already been declared. We lost.

Captivity

She asked to see down there
and I complied.
She wore a nurse's uniform
but reminded me of my mother.
Down there can seem so far away.
Down there is another world.

When she inserted the tube
I thought I'd scream
I licked the tip of my nose
and sucked my lip.
I hid my face.
She held my cock like it was an
engagement ring.

She saw the fear in my eyes
and understood.
Hospitals turn us all into
little girls. There are no men
in the wards. Our cocks withdraw.
They loll and cringe like snails.
It's no time for heroics,
no place for a boner.

How much pee can there be?
Enough to fill the bag, doctor
says. She smiled when she
came in again, this time to remove
the tube. I bit the mattress.
Coming out proved more painful
than going in, possibly like a poison
arrow. I asked for a slug of whiskey
and emitted a deep sigh.

The hospital staff could have been Sioux
but sounded like Comanche. First,
they stripped me naked. Next, they stained
my body with yellow dye. The Medicine Man
cut me open and shoved long objects into my veins.
He asked me questions and demanded answers.
Finally, tawny braves carried me back. Squaws
applied salves and potions. When I woke,
the Chief and the village council stood
at the foot of my bed to welcome me back
from the land of no tomorrows.

One rarely sleeps in a lobby.
One is unlikely to head out
without one's undershorts and pants.
Bottomless is strictly for the birds and little tots.
I had ten experts come to inspect my crotch.
It left me a changed man.
It is odd to be reduced to flesh.
Nobody asks in a hospital what one thinks.
One is not in a knife fight; one hasn't got a chance.
The incisions are terrifying. As the pins go in,
one becomes a specimen, a patient etherized,
a monarch butterfly.
Some keep their eyes open.
I closed mine.

Hallelujah Trail

People brag about the religious experiences.
They feel something, they tell us,
when they're taking a crap. But
they won't go to church.

Baseball, they say, is a kind of religion.
They are believers. Some are truer
than others; they tell us that, too.
Why can't they just use the toilet?

Others like to fornicate in the pews.
They're in search of religion, they
tell us. They don't find it when
praying, but they are true believers.
Call them devout. Their theatre
is the Broadway musical. The priest:
Al Jolson. Last year: Sinatra.
These days: Lady Gaga.

They're gamblers. They don't like
religion, they tell us. Spirituality,
yes, that. They're very spiritual,
especially when their stocks
are rising. They're very spiritual
but they love money.

They don't like the institution. They
like to sleep around, too. They're
against marriage, but they're
into true love. They prefer it free
since it's so valuable. If they
can't have it, they'll take it.
They'll give it away, too, often
to the highest bidder.

This generation of malcontents and
rebels will say anything to feel better.
They'd learn to play the xylophone if they
could play stoned. They're stumbling
through grad school and got low marks
in 3rd grade. They're catching up
now but never studied Latin.

They walk around with their
mouths hanging open.
They complain a lot, especially
when their coffee isn't hot.
They pride themselves on their
needs. When they're passed over
at the audition, they storm out,
cursing. They'll never sing again.

They threaten now to take
their grievances to the street.
It's high noon. The kids without a future
hope to be noticed. The entire world
is like Schwab's Drug Store.
Maybe they'll be seen crying at
the counter and be cast as
zombies in next year's
blockbuster. They have lots of
experience. They can play the part.
All they have to do is look
vacant.

Poetry: Buy, Sell or Hold?

I sent my new poem to an old friend who replied:
"I know nothing of poetry."
Another said about the same. "I don't read the stuff.
Sorry." It got me to thinking.

Had I sent a stock tip, they would have rewarded me.
I might have received a bottle of Chablis, maybe even a
good one, had I sent trading data on Nasdaq or the New
York Stock Exchange. Who would have said, "I'm not into
making money."?

But one comes to learn an awful truth about one's friends.
Not just their indifference; that's painful enough.
No. It's that for them poetry is something akin to
masturbation. They don't want to hear about it.
It's an embarrassment.

My friends are always buying or selling. If I had produced
a tomato, I'd have been advised to set up a stand on the
sidewalk. The price of tomatoes is high, asparagus even
higher. But poetry is nearly worthless; like trying to sell
one's underwear.

Poetry is not a commodity. My friends are merchants.
It's a shameful action, like going to confession.
Can you sell your sins? How much do one's dreams weigh?
Nobody wants to watch a friend display himself.

It's not that poetry is disgusting. But it may be shameful.
It's seen as a waste of time. Not an adult activity, not a
good investment. Something akin to gathering pine cones
or pressing leaves in an album, i.e., kid stuff, or a hobby for
little old ladies.

I feel like a cat taking a bloody mouse to her master.
As I drop my poem at my friend's feet, she gives it a glance
and sneers: "What's that for? It's not very pleasant.
Your job is to please me. Go play in the garden."

That's the response of my once best friend. She sees herself
as an artist or at least as artistic. She wouldn't treat a
painting the way she scorns poetry. But then again you can
own an oil. You can hang it. Even better you can resell it.

Stocks and paintings are good investments, like real estate.
Cars and furniture lose value, more like poetry. They're
best when new, but with art, the worth is in its place, they
say. It's not just beauty; it's location, location, location.

Poetry is a dying art, especially when the artistic scorn it.
They'd rather have crème brûlée or pear mousse with
walnuts. It's not only prettier but something sweet. Poetry
is no treat, and poets are a nuisance. They have the absurd
idea that what they do has value.

Street Theatre

The news tonight is that there are rioters rioting in the streets of Charlotte. I want to be a witness; I'll go myself.

I see folks on the pavement and they look like they are having a riot but they say to me they are dancers dancing not rioters rioting and I believe them. One of them points out that the proof they are dancing is that they are having a good time. If they were rioting they wouldn't be happy.

I have to confess to not having thought of that, that dancers are happy while rioters are otherwise. That makes a lot of sense to me. Dancers do tend to be happy, I can say with some certainty; I know this because I too have done some dancing, but I really know little about rioting.

I go next to one of the ushers, a large man in a blue uniform. He's wearing a helmet. I figure he must work for the theatre. First thing, I ask if I need a ticket. He, too, seems happy, because he bursts out laughing. He says I must be joking. Don't I know matinees are free?

This cheers me immensely. Had I known beforehand, I tell the usher, I could have invited my girlfriend or even my parents. I notice then that the usher is carrying a pistol. I've been in theatres around the world, in Tokyo, London, and even Moscow, but I have never seen an usher carrying a loaded weapon. When I see that, I decide not to ask for a program. I think I'd better move on. I wonder if the ushers are having trouble controlling the audience. They are unruly.

I start walking toward the sunken stage and public auditorium. It is crowded so I figure that like the other folks I might have to settle for standing room only.

I want a seat in the orchestra but I notice that there are really no bad seats. I already have a great view.

The dancers are clearly in the middle of a scene. I must have missed the opening. They are shouting and swirling, kicking their legs and waving banners and posters. One is burning the flag. I can't quite make out what they are saying. I figure they are doing some sort of medieval pageant, a festival, or perhaps even a wedding.

One thing I keep hearing is "it matters, it matters" (what matters?) and then almost in unison I catch something like "don't shoot." I decide then that I must be watching a modern version of *Romeo and Juliet*, which happens to be a favorite. It looks to have an almost entirely Afro-American cast, which I think is a neat innovation. I like creative casting. I must have walked in on the fight scene, because the actors are very excited.

Anyway, I am having a ball and so, it seems, is the rest of the audience. I can't wait to read the reviews. The Charlotte paper used to have a great theatre critic, but now just a string of people who write about what's called entertainment. But this is great, real public theatre right downtown in the business district. The city is finally getting its act together.

Guns and Roses

Who's afraid of Virginia Woolf? Cried the playwright.
Who shot the sheriff? Asked the singer. The next question
to pose is this: who signed up for this: — classrooms
without teachers, cars without drivers, politicians at each
other's throats? Are we all in the same boat or are some of
us in the water? They are bashing us with their paddles. It's
sink or swim. We've got girls digging trenches, gays
aiming bazookas. The drones killing our enemies. Bombs at
the ready. The people don't want freedom? We'll blow
them to smithereens.

We accept cookies. The end is inevitable.
In Texas, people say howdy; in Maine, it's strictly hi there.
It's gotten so, some call this diversity of opinion.
As long as we all agree on what's important,
as long as we say fuck you but not nigger, it will all be fine.
As long as we vote for the same person and with passion,
dance to the same music, run with the pack; as long as we
don't smoke, we can proceed to checkout.

After all, we're all the same, isn't that true?
We're all humans, all equal beings.
The only difference is that we're better than them.
We are because we know more, we do more,
and we're a whole lot cleaner. Humans are equal;
it's that we do the right thing, but they won't.
The people we hate are the uncouth and the tacky.
Otherwise, people are fine. I especially
love blacks. Soon there will be one human race.
Hurray!

What I am getting at is this: Gertrude Stein was right all
along. Roses are roses are roses, that's true.
But does a rose grown without soil have

65

fragrance? I'm told not. We'll get our bouquet,
as promised, petals at our feet, our welcome home, our
victory parade after the defeat of our enemies. But
without their sweet aroma, what good are roses?
When everything else is the color and odor of blood,
what use are flowers?

Manufactured

We blocked the road with snow mounds,
and pelted drivers with balls of ice.
We threw corn nuts on the roads
to attract mockingbirds and crows.
At Christmas we unscrewed decorative lights
from neighbors' doors and windows,
and smashed them in the street. We left wreaths
alone and pissed in the snow. We called it fun.

The elevators at the Century Building
were open by day. We ran in hoping
for a ride to the top of the world.
Alas, the secretaries chased us back out
into the bright sun, promising to call 911.
Next we headed for Krystal's for a 10-cent burger;
a chocolate shake or fries was a dime more.
All of this was bliss in July at 95 degrees in the shade.

The bridge was too far so we stayed where we were,
just east of the Mississippi in Shelby, stuck forever
between the zoo and Beale. When we got bored,
which was every other day, we went out in the yard with
daggers. We burned each other's toes and plotted trips to
the dogs. The English bull dog humped our legs while the
Afghan hounds raced us through the bushes. We ate potato
chips at midnight and cried: we'll go back tomorrow. We
were too excited to sleep.

Sunday school was just a racket; we could see
through it all with their picked-over donuts and stale coffee.
What we wanted was adventure, racing off to leer at
drawings of pussy and tits in crayon on the walls of storm
drains, throwing 4th of July firecrackers in November,

or bicycling to the worm factory behind the Police
Academy. After dark, we hunted for smashed cola cups at
the ball park and clung in the parking lot to the hoods of
passing cars.

I for one feel sorry that it's all been taken away
for no good reason. All our memories up in smoke.
We're required instead to dance to the threat of
insurrection. Hip hop is the music of indoctrination; we
preferred rock or soul or the blues; Furry Lewis got our
attention when he played at the Shell. The Old Forest
full of heavy growth lures us back but all we find is an
empty lot, a ghost town called invention.

Hudson Canvas

We all live on the Hudson, America's only true river. It's a driveway, a landing strip, and a dead end. The Hudson is not the only river to become a school, but it is the only one once beheld by the likes of George Washington, Melville, and Sir Winston Churchill. The Hudson is a work of art surrounded by cathedrals first seen by Thomas Cole, Church, and Cropsey. It is the river of Allen Ginsberg and Malcolm X. The Hudson crosses the country from the Atlantic to the Pacific, linking Boston to San Francisco. Look at a map.

The Hudson doesn't only contain water; it embodies all that is known and then some. It holds the land. It encircles the earth. West Point, that cool cat school where men train to remain calm under fire, lies in the river valley, in Cheever country, where his swimmer drank until he lost track of where he was going. Hyde Park to the north, Yonkers to the south: lose one's way and end up in the Bronx, not far from that immortal stadium, just up from Maya Angelou's Harlem. Not as far west as Buffalo, not as far east as the Berkshires, where Edith Wharton once made guests feel cosmopolitan.

Somewhere in the Connecticut forests can be found the best: Philip Roth standing at his desk, concocting stories of lust and loss, not far from Bellow's Hudson, where he trained lions. There they lived in the shadow of their depression-era hero, FDR, who stuffed bird carcasses and dreamt of flying. They lived by the pen in the shadow of that river, from Peekskill to Newark, bought and paid for in its youth, once owned by Cornelius Vanderbilt, a man not taken in by Huck Finn's brand of jive.

The Nile might be longer but this eerie canal runs deeper. The Hudson's not only a river but an artery. It's the life blood of this nation. Unlike the Mississippi, the Hudson doesn't flood. It runs full force into the sea. It takes its time and then picks up at Poughkeepsie. It's not called ol' man river because it's young and feminine. A real dame, she minds her own business. The tears of the Iroquois add to the river's flow. They're what give the river depth. The Amazon runs black, filled with piranha and cashew husks, but the Hudson feeds on pine and beaver fur, English blue bloods, and greedy Dutch.

The Hudson runs through steel country, not rubber plantations, navigated by men dressed in black, not adventurers in panama hats. This river, an aqua duct of despair and hope, now runs clear. FDR's backyard has been spared. Vanderbilt's ships are gone; the river prevails. It is New York's longest running show, surpassing Broadway Baby by a millennium. Its lights never dim. Sharks can't swim upstream. Corn floats. This river flows to the base of the Statue of Liberty. It soaks up the ashes of burning buildings. Corpses float to the bottom. Debris is carried out to sea. The Hudson will always be a safe spot to land.

Indecent Exposure

Memphis is on the Mississippi,
but nobody knows how to leave.
The horizon is on the other side of the river,
but nobody dares cross that bridge.
We are stay-at-home types, little chickens.
Everything in Memphis is thought the best.
I was taught the art gallery in the park
was bigger and better than the Met.
Second rate is not just good enough,
it is embraced, hailed as fine.
"Who do you think you are?"

When we were kids, we ate chow mein from a can.
We put butter on our white rice. We thought sliced bread
was a thing of wonder. We salted our watermelon.
Some of us were racists. Some still are.

When I was 12, my best friend Matt was accused
of having combed his pubes. The boys at school almost
drove him to suicide. I was told at a middle-school party to
stand up and kiss my so-called girlfriend on the lips, but
that year at age 13 I didn't know how or why.
I stood in the middle of the room and died.
One day I was singing the lyrics to the Stones'
"Satisfaction" as I entered class. One of the girls sniffed,
"How would you know?" If you were not a stud, you were
a dud. I felt surrounded by wolves. It's a miracle I survived
or maybe I didn't. I still can't sleep at night. I still wet my
bed.

And yet when I look back I wonder how I ever left.
I left so much behind. I gave up all that for this.
I gave up Faulkner for *Vogue.*

I gave up the blues for rap. Shit, I gave up barbeque for tacos. I gave up everything I knew for the unknown. It is still unknown. It will always be so. I will always be lost. I will never find my way home.

Making Trouble

Don't you know the difference between a potato and a lion?

That's odd.

They put lions on pajamas but not potatoes. You'll never see potatoes on your brother's pajamas.

Lions roar. Lions are not called spuds. Lions are fine and dandy, like petunias or dandelions. Your mother could make potato and dandelion soup, if she cared to, and you could help.

All you'd need is a dandy lion and an ideal potato.

Potatoes grow on trees. Just tell your favorite farmer you'll need a bushel this year. He'll know what to do. But they'll be fewer apples if he grows potatoes. You'll have to think it through.

Of course, some say potatoes don't grow on trees. Some people get quite angry about this mistake. My father used to shout, "You're always forgetting to turn out the lights. Do you think potatoes grow on trees?"

When I was young, we were poor. Father would turn over the ketchup bottle to catch the very last drop. My family liked to put ketchup on our potatoes, but not on our lions. Ketchup grows on trees, too. Put in your order at the start of the year.

But when it comes to lions, I'd be careful. I wouldn't get too close. Lions are reluctant to swim. You're probably thinking of dolphins who can swim very fast. They swim as fast as crows can fly. But I wouldn't put ketchup on the crows either. In point of fact, you'd be better off keeping the ketchup to yourself.

So, where were we? You've got the ketchup, the lion, and the potato, not to mention the dolphins and the lights. What are we forgetting? The crows! And the trees. Don't forget to turn off the trees. And the apple sauce. If there is any left.

Now pick the petunias before it is too late. Add them to the soup. Stir. When it comes to the boil, you'll have chicken soup. Enjoy. (Serves 4.)

French Revolution

It's all about the money, not the population.

Let's revert to the camp fires.
We'll take up flints and arrows.
We'll make spears and pierce the heart of this so-called art.
Smash it all; shred it; throw it into the sea.

My friend Keisha McCormick took one look at Mark
Rothko's *Void #3* and wanted to vomit. She redoubled her
gaze. "I look at this painting but can't find my people. I
only see you." Where, she demanded, are my African-
American brothers and sisters?

This is not part of my people. We're not at the center;
we're not even at the side. Why must I study this pervert
style? This is not Mississippi. The sexes may be mingling,
but the races are splitting. In future, Kanye West must be
shown at the side of Leonardo's Mona Lisa.

We are radical practitioners of right thinking, determined to
destroy Western Civilization. We must step back to move
forward: first go the arts and the Decorations, then the
courts, the laws and institutions. By the time we're
Through, they'll be nothing left but vaginal jelly
and sawed-off shotguns.

If I can't see my people, I want to get rid of it as Genghis
Khan and the Taliban dynamited Bamiyan. We'll destroy
the offending statuary. Why should a museum be a
sanctuary? We are determined to enact our purity.
There can be no beauty without justice.

You give us our cut. 13% or we'll burn the art, set the
museums on fire. We're kind-hearted, loving and caring,
but you give us the sculpture or we'll cut your necks.

Oprah goes right up on that Sistine Chapel with Louis
Farrakhan and Michael Jackson. Until that day, that's
nothing but another ugly ceiling.

Guernica? The Prado, what's that got to do with it?
Why's that horse's neck cut in two? Picasso use a
guillotine? He's as much a sadist as an artist. I'd call that
horse a gelding. How can the symbol of human suffering be
depicted by animal mutilation?

It is not just about renaming Yale after Malcolm.
We must demolish the Washington Monument.
We burn with righteous resentment. My parents only make
$229,000 a year. They can afford to send me to college but
can't buy me an Audi.

Put this shit in a vault, send it to the university archives.
Who wants to see Chippewa or Oneida paddling bark
canoes? Subservience to white settlers is offensive. This art
depicts a race-based view. Those offended have declared it
harmful. The First Amendment is racist.

This country needs new style of art. How about renaming
the Grand Tetons? Or Michelle and President Obama, both
nude, placed in a golden chariot? They'd look cool next to
Lady Liberty. That's what I'm saying.
Where is the people's eternal flame?

It's all about the money, not the population.

Next Door Neighbor

The man who moans
moans because he lives alone.
His moans are not the same
as the couple upstairs.
Say no more.

He moans because he is still alive.
His moans are like sighs.
They communicate isolation. It's
the human equivalent of an owl's hoo.
Almost like boo hoo. But not quite.

The guy's lonely.

When the young men are lonely,
they whistle.
The man who moans can't whistle,
but he wants company.
He's lonely.

When we hear moaning, we
feel discomfort. Humans recognize
despair. It's in our genes.
It's coming and we know it.
It's basic.

In the meantime, we laugh.
Or whatever. You don't hear
a lot of moaning from the young.
Nor from the young at heart.
It's disturbing.

A whistle is a mating call.
The young man wants company.

He expresses appreciation, however
awkwardly, however rudely. It's
base, but it's sexy.
Women secretly love it.
Dying men don't whistle.

The dying want company
but not sexual attention.
Sex is the furthest thing
from the mind of the man
who moans. He's alone.

The penis no longer works. It
doesn't even perform its
primary function, which
is pissing. Even that is an ordeal.

Hey, this is real.

The man moans for all that's gone,
including his once sharp mind.

The ease of pissing goes first,
then the brain.
The combination is discouraging.
You can't piss and you can't remember
where you laid your glasses.

Some cry.

I never do. I moan.

Outer Space

Jason has disappeared from my vision.
Then there's Michael.
Marian is gone, then mom and dad.
One by one they go.
Soon: no one.

I feel like the man on the moon.
The astronaut left to drift, holding
his severed umbilical cord, gasping;
earth at a distance, disappearing.
I'm going, getting smaller and smaller.

I'm saying hello but no one can hear me.
Like Marilyn Monroe or Cher's husband,
Sonny. Lost in space, the movie. It
opens in September.
Lost forever, the nightmare: 24/7.

I've arrived at the lost and found,
but I can't remember what I came for.
Sign here.

There were once so many;
I could name them but why bother?
Some leads, but mainly a chorus, a jubilee, not a party.
More like a camp fire without marshmallows.
A cookout, without charcoal; a broken nail with no file.
Tits without ass. A pocket with no money.

How the hell did it happen?
Oh, it's one decision after the other.
Choices.
Ingratiation, followed by despair.
Indoctrination, then disappointment.

It's leaving home in a hurry.
It's a flat tire on the highway.
It's a bridge too far.
Emasculation.

It's not 2+2=4.
It's not oppression, not control.
Not intervention, not suppression,
not even repression, no.
It's indifference.
The tyranny of neglect.
It's choking on nothing.
It's a phone call to We Care,
only We Care is moving.
Call back tomorrow.
By the time you get through,
your problems are over.
Leave your name after the beep.
By the time you get through,
it's been settled.
Press 'O' for operator assistance.
By the time you get through,
you're finished.
How may we direct your call?

Confessions of a Bad Driver

I am a man, too.
Listen up.
I've given up.
I'm one of those guys who never wins.
I have no backing.
I've never been in the right place at the right time.
I've never been elected.
I've never been called to the microphone.
My shoes are often left untied.
I forget to zip my fly.
No one has ever said to me, "I love you."

I missed out on disco-mania.
I still use too much salt.
I smoke.
I hit my children.
I ate canned ravioli as a kid.
My life is almost over.
I won't let my wife serve instant rice.
I often forget to lift the seat.
I don't know how to tie a tie.
I never take down my Christmas lights.
My mother called me stupid.

I bite my nails.
I have a pimply ass.
I forget to flush.
I voted for Richard Nixon.
I make my wife take out the garbage.
I can't catch a ball.
My wife makes me sleep in the den.
She says I smell like a dead mouse.
My first grade teacher said I should be ashamed of myself.
My high school coach said I was full of shit.

My father beat my ass.

I have no friends.
I hate the snow.
I used to eat Lucky Charms.
I love baseball.
I've changed a lot of flat tires.
I never look at porno.
I used to like cutting the grass.
I joined the boycott against Coca Cola.
I've never been out of state.
I voted for Ronald Reagan.
I voted for Bush.

I once hated the Soviet Union.
I hated communists like Jane Fonda.
I hated the Viet Cong.
Now I love the Taliban.
I'm not into hate.
I didn't take Watergate seriously.
I didn't vote for Obama.
I always order broccoli beef and spring rolls at the Chink's.
I drive a Chevy.
I'd like to retire to Panama.
I laughed when my brother got hit in the head by a fly ball.

I'm a goner.
I won't let my wife shave her pussy.
I prefer sunflowers to roses.
I am an alcoholic.
My wife had her left tit removed.
I've always wanted to see the Pyramids.
I think Pete Rose got shafted.
I voted for Trump.
I've never been to a French restaurant.
I never go to church.

I think Margaret Thatcher had balls.

God bless America.

The Artist's Touch

Artists refuse to tell us why
what we do every day is drudgery,
but for them, joy. They love
what they do, they declare, but
they know we dig the same holes
with a sense of woe. We're
dying but they thrive. What
we do is called work, but for
them it is more…it is
something entirely different.
It's a kick and they are rewarded
for it. They sell the holes they dig.
They're able to see in the dark.
They can go about barefooted or
drive a car without a license.
In their world a toilet is not
merely a throne; it's a rack for
sombreros, a podium for speeches,
and, if not that, then an umbrella stand
for tomatoes.

But putting objects to use is not
the sole talent of artists. Anyone can do that.
No, their talent includes the ability
to wrest power. Their skill involves
class warfare. They've managed
near and far to disenchant the gentry,
to rob the ruling class of its glamour.
Everyone wants to be Picasso, not the Duke
of Devon. The planter class in Mississippi
has been displaced by Elvis. Nobody
thinks the Taylors, the McFaddens,
or Walker Percy's family are anything special.
People want to meet the poet in his garret,

not the lord of the manor, however grand
his six thousand acres may be. Women threw
themselves at Dylan Thomas, not at Nelson Rockefeller.
Tiny Tim counts, but not the Queen's poorer cousins.
Madonna holds court, as did Andy Warhol. David Bowie
is imagined to have something to say, but not
the little old lady from Pasadena.

An entire class has been displaced by singer
song writers and horny painters. One thinks of Lucien
Freud and Francis Bacon with their paint brushes.
They have more in common with stable
boys than aristocrats, but are much more likely
to be called milord and greeted with applause
than some eccentric landowner with a six-car garage.
Artists did that, not the French Revolution,
and don't you forget it. "Madame Bovary" lives.
Charles Bukowski appears in Sean Penn's dreams.
Movie stars love his vomit. Even dreck has cachet.
Even the Chinese value Rothko. Hitler knew not to
bomb Paris. American pilots steered clear
of Kyoto. And it wasn't to save gas.

This is why the world was shocked when the Americans
left the Baghdad Museum unguarded, not by the bombing
of civilians. In modern times, you can incinerate the people,
but one mustn't abandon the Titian. J. Paul Getty
valued Fabergé Eggs, not herds of cattle. Art is life. Today,
Elvis's shorts lie beneath protective glass guarded by the
sheriff. His landlord's underwear was given to charity.
The same thing applies to Japan and Brazil:
stars are from the country, not the countryside. Get out
there and claim your hole. Put a circle around it
and name it. Modern art is about making something
from nothing. Artists are nobodies, not has-beens.
They belong to tomorrow.

Cash and Carry

It's the middle class that celebrates congestion.
Millionaires prefer land.
The rich in America buy ranches; elsewhere: estates.
Our movie stars move to Montana. There's a reason.
The rich know something we don't know?
I doubt it. We all secretly want to get out.
We dream of escape. Our hypocrisy is easy
to see through. Nobody wants to deal with the flow.
It's a lie that we love the crowds.
The masses scare us; this is what explains Beverly Hills.

People need a way out. Humanity requires too much
attention. The floods send us running; we head for higher
ground. Nothing is more disheartening than a crowded
beach. We associate it with failure. Hot dogs lose their taste
when we look out on to a sea of people.
Suddenly the sight of flesh is a turn off.
Fatty legs and pink bellies are a fright. Tits become tits.
Massive muscles make men look like bulls.

The stink of our fellow man drives us on.
One can't wait to get out. Turn up the radio and hit the
road. Home sweet home becomes an adventure.
What an escape. Sartre was right; other people are hell.
This is what's behind capitalism; not greed.
It's desperation. The dream of solitude.
A deep, abiding, instinctive recognition that little good
can come from living too close to others. Neighbors are
great when they are far away.

Missing

What's missing?
Absolutely everything, dad, absolutely everything,
including you.

Who's missing?

I have friends who don't sleep at night.
Are they thinking of what's happened or worried about
tomorrow?

The ball came this close but missed my head.
It's called a close call.
All of life is a close call, mother said.

Who, what, where, when, why, how?

Mother's left breast is missing.
Does she miss it? Did he?

Humes. Clover. Des Moines, Iowa. Coldspring.
There's no tomorrow and yesterday's forgotten.

You will be missed means you're still alive.
You're not dead yet but you will be.
Welcome to your funeral.

Is anything missing?
There is something missing but I can't put my finger on it.

My front tooth is missing.
I missed the bus.
Mom's purse.
Where's my sock?

No, I don't miss the bus.

I missed the boat.

"I'll teach you to talk that way to your mother!"
You missed.
"I won't miss next time."
There won't be a next time, father.

There never is a next time.

I miss you.

What's Done Cannot Be Un-Done

On the death of a fellow citizen at the hands of a lunatic
leader, Mr. Kim Jong-un of North Korea,
let it be said I protest. Vengeance is not wrong,
but vengeance is not enough. Anger has its place and,
rightly, a place of honor, but anger is not the way, oh no,
not yet; It's not Pearl Harbor. If you can cry for Argentina,
you can cry for Otto Warmbier. Where's Madonna?

We're pissed off about dear Otto, and rightly so.
Un did it, but he can't un-do it. What's done is done.
It's un-acceptable to seek vengeance; it's un-American
to strike back just for fun, just to get even; that would be
un-Acceptable. We'll leave that to the World Court. We'll
refer Mr. Un, the fat sadist, to the UN. If you can cry for
Argentina, you can cry for Otto Warmbier. Where's Dennis
Rodman?

Un can speak at the podium. The UN will no doubt
welcome him as a friend. Un will be greeted by applause,
perhaps even a standing ovation by his fellow
thugs. Putin might even give Un a hug. The Presidents of
Iran, Venezuela, Cuba and Zimbabwe will make him feel
right at home; they might even give him a medal.
But not our Ambassador; she knows better. She won't be
applauding basketball fan and supreme leader, Kim Jong-
un. If you can cry for Argentina, you can cry
for Otto Warmbier. Where's Nancy Pelosi?

Our President is un-happy. Meanwhile, Congress dithers.
The Democrats sweat. They're not sure if murder of an
American citizen is wrong. After all, according to
Mr. Un, young Otto did something wrong. He may have
deserved it. The Democrats are un-believable. Some are un-
patriotic. Congress will wait for instructions from CNN.

Only Trump knows what to do. He won't wait to have his say. Trump will not delay. Un's done. If you can cry for Argentina, you can cry for Otto Warmbier. Where's Chuck Schumer now?

World Class

I.   **Substitute Teaching**

In America, acting is frowned on.
People are looking for passion.
People want to know how much you care.
They expect burn-out.

Two years of hard work is all anyone can manage.
You give your all; you'll be a star.
They want you to put yourself at their mercy.
Then crash and burn.
Everyone understands.

The students in turn will do nothing. It's not expected.
Students are praised for being born. They want a prize.
They want to be rewarded for living.
They want to be thanked for coming.
They'd prefer to be paid.

Your job is not to act like a teacher, but to be a friend.
If they don't like you, you'll be blamed.
If you just act like a friend, the kids will laugh.
Even the Principal will advise against your trying to be a
teacher.

Teachers, after all, make and enforce rules. Your success
will be measured by your willingness to make exceptions.
Waive the rules. Overlook the cheating. Pass those who are
failing. Teachers who act like teachers are hated.

Act like a teacher, and the students will turn on you.
You'll do best to pretend. Act like a student. You're one of
them. You too are a kid. You too smoke pot. You too like
porn. You too have a tattoo. Be cool. Show the boys and

girls you're real. Open your pants. Do handstands. Now
you're cooking. You'll get the hang of it.
Believe it or not, they pay you to act the fool.
Smile. Say you're sorry. You'll be fine…for a time.

II.   Kabuki Lessons

Japanese praise role-playing above all else.
If the teacher acts like a teacher, and looks like a teacher,
he is deemed to be a teacher. Dress the part. Polish your
shoes. Students take their cue from the act. If you act like a
teacher, they will in turn act like students.

This has nothing to do with teaching, of course,
and nothing to do with learning. The act is the outcome.
The performance is what is rated, not the applause.
There are no gods of caring. Passion is frowned upon.
You're expected to come in everyday for the duration of
your career.

That's what teachers do. Caring too much is seen as a sign
of malfeasance, a possible illness. You can teach your heart
out, but if you leave early, they'll call you lazy.
Interference is a form of molestation. You don't call the
parents when daughter forgets her homework. You don't
call the police if she comes in with bruises. You mind your
own business.

People will wonder why you care, and she better not be
cute. If you talk to the boys, they'll figure you're a homo.
They'll be concerned. Stand back, and do your job. Your
job is to go through the motions. Attend commencement,
accept flowers at graduation, smile.

Don't laugh or cry, that's not professional.
Look busy; you don't have to do anything.

Don't complain. Don't offer suggestions for improvements. Don't talk about student needs. Come in at 7 and leave after 5. You'll do fine. Don't whine.

Prepare to be surprised: My top engineering student aged 19 asked me why all Americans eat McDonald's, breakfast, lunch and dinner, seven days a week. "Don't you get tired of eating the same thing?" "Do you have fish in your rivers?" "Have you ever eaten rice?" Tell them you're dying to try. Smile.

III.　　Great Wall of China

And then there's China, our "enemy." I've taught there, too. They come to class looking for escape from the State.

They are sick of fake news. At the same time, they're doing college math in 6th grade. They're easily bored. They read Jane Austin in English.

Their favorite movie is "Roman Holiday" with Audrey Hepburn. They figure you know something. Of course, they value kindness and patience.

They value excitement most of all, challenge, being asked to work harder. They are willing to pull all-nighters every day of the year.

They'll assume you're easy because you're lazy. They won't like you for doing nothing. In fact, they'll hate you.

They like passion. It's a novelty. They like to be scared. They love Japanese horror movies.

They don't think being stupid is funny.
They associate ignorance with hunger not with laughter.

They're ambitious. They want to know why you gave them
a 98 and not a 99. They won't be willing to let it go.
They're eager-beavers.

They think government propaganda is boring,
But they want most of all to die for their country.

They're in a struggle to become number one.
They want to take over. They're desperate to win, I'd say.

They figure you've come to the right place to teach.
China is hot.

IV.   Chalk Dust and Sand

What about the Arabs, you ask. Yes, I once taught in Saudi
Arabia.
This is very difficult to answer. Arab males I know, not
females. Never met one.
The boys are willing to study but would prefer to wheel and
deal. "My average," one lad said, "may be 67, but, teacher,
my friend, I'll need 80 to pass. For me, just this time, won't
you help?"

If you say no, he will excuse himself and walk away.
If you say yes, he will kiss your feet and promise life-long
loyalty. In either case, he will forget all about it in less than
a minute. If you get the reputation for never bending, they
will say you black-hearted. If you get the reputation of
always bending, they will call you a fool.

Somehow or other, your goal is to be known for having a
white soul.

For Arabs, they'll respect your brain, but they'll love your
heart. Justice means nothing to them; they want mercy.
They won't ask you to be fair. They will beg you for a
favor. There is no such thing as rules in the desert,
just love. They want you to love them and, if you do, they
will love you back.

It is in my experience very easy to love them, but it is not
easy to teach them. Here are a few tips: Don't ask them
what they want. Their reply will be, "As you like, teacher.
Suit yourself" Deciding is your job, not theirs.
They won't give input. They don't want responsibility.
They know nothing of democracy. They don't want to vote.

They assume you know what you are doing. If you don't,
they'll complain. It's not manly to grovel, to seek
cooperation. Fathers don't do that. The King doesn't ask
permission; he wouldn't stoop to it. It'll be tough
if you are an American, but you'll have to act like a man.
You decide. They'll ask why, but the answer can be
"because I said so."

They know no fear. You can't threaten them. You have
little to give and little they want. But they'll study to make
you happy. They'll study for their mothers.
They'll ask if you like them, but they'll already know the
answer. They are hyper-sensitive like rattle-snakes. They'll
feel your pain. "Teacher," one boy said to me,
"if you cry, we will cry." They are sly like a fox. They'll
give you a lot to cry about.

They will obey or not. Deal with it. At a deep, deep level,
nothing really matters. They know that God doesn't care
much about such things. At some level, they think nothing
matters. They'll submit to God but not to you.

They'll skip their finals to visit a friend in hospital with an
ingrown toenail. They are the opposite of ambitious.
They'd happily pay a Filipino to do their work.

They'd happily bribe you to give them an "A." Your job is
to survive somehow without becoming resentful. I wouldn't
call it education as such; I'd call it training. Whatever
happens, you'll be blamed. You'll be praised
for nothing. There's very little Arabs expect from Infidels.
They figure you have little to give. After 6 years, I
concluded they were right.

Abomination of Good Cheer

Write something cheerful, advises
my dear cousin from the early
seventeenth-century, a wretched
girl born in a nondescript town-house
down on New Amsterdam's Wall Street. Write
something less depressing, something
perhaps about gladioli or parmesan
cheese, please, she begs.

In those days, 14th Street was
Uptown. I should know. That's
not too far from where the
Van Valkenburgh homestead was first staked
out, some 400 years ago. That's
before women with wide bottoms
were body shamed and long before
men dared walk the streets hand
in hand like adolescent girls.
There was cow shit everywhere and
without a candle you had to sit
in the dark.

It was long ago. Back, back before
yesterday, when porcupines
ruled the waves. Back in the day,
as tattooed youths in bright, bleached
T-shirts say today, back before girls
gave blow-jobs for lunch money,
back before singers with gold-capped
teeth sang songs about shooting
bitches, when people lived in harmony
or tried to, and if they didn't,
were shunned or driven off.

The Dutch settlers now are
largely forgotten. The Van Burens
and Roosevelts seem almost
quaint, just memories like Anastasia and the
Russian Tsar; there aren't even any photos.
One thinks of churning butter or, perhaps
of FDR's stuffed birds. It was a long time ago
when the Dutch occupied the Hudson Valley;
long ago when they built their fort
on lower Manhattan. Who cares?
Now we dream of holidays
in the South Pacific: topless
girls and venereal disease.
Melville prevails.

But cheer up. There's nothing wrong
that a little life can't cure.
Think of sunflowers, think of John Coltrane,
not boll weevils. Remember the Alamo,
not the Holocaust. The American dream
carries on, ever-expanding, evolving. The
Dutch came and went. It's all been
left in good hands. We stand
now blindfolded, ready to walk
the plank. The pirates are not
simpletons. They're brothers and
sisters; they're gung-ho. They just
want justice. Let the purge begin.
We'll declare ourselves obsolete. Their
leaders read the comics; their rallying cry
is familiar: quack, quack, quack. Could
anything be more encouraging
than ducks on a mission?

Tokyo Express

That man there used to be my father.
I recognize those blue-veined arms on that corpse riding the
train with me from Shimokitazawa to Chitose-Funabashi.
That's the corpse of my father, I swear to God.

I recognize his receding hairline and his pale skin.
It even has curly hair and wears glasses. That's dad,
all right, sitting there beneath the sign for special seating.
That's exactly where he'd sit if he were alive.

Dad saw himself as disabled and in some ways he was.
He was an emotional cripple, that's for sure.
He flew into rages over nothing.

I once got up the courage to point out there were no other
cars on the road but he was cursing. He was ranting. He
looked out the window and stopped. When I was eleven,
he'd have turned around and smacked me on the head. He
was always threatening to trounce me.

Dad was a bully. When I was little, mother asked me to get
dad an aspirin to go with his pickled herring and his dry
martini. Years later, dad once said, "After two martinis, I'm
not afraid of anything." I like that.

Like a lot of monsters, he had a heart of gold. Like
Frankenstein and all his monster friends, he scared the
neighborhood children but felt lonely. Like many bullies
before him, what he needed was a blind man to make
him a cup of tea. It was precisely because people were not
blind that he hated them.

Oh, but how well Edward Albee understood him. What he
wanted above all else was love: L.O.V.E. Just like an

alcoholic, but he didn't drink. No, his father drank enough
for two generations. He once said, "You think you're a big
shot, but you're nothing but a big shit." I like that, too. I
used to pick cashews out from father's dish of mixed nuts.
Amazingly, it didn't make him mad. It amused him.
I did that from his lap.

That old Japanese guy sitting across from me reminds me
of my father when he was alive. The old man there looks
very thoughtful, looks intelligent. My father, too, had that
look. I wish I did.

That man's flesh is as white as a frog's belly, so pale I can
see his blue cheesy veins. I could see my father's, too. It
made him look frail. He'd get cross but with no power. He
became pathetic, especially when he smelled of urine.

It's hard to control other people when you stink.
It's impossible to run the show when you've sprung a leak.
It's hard to frighten your son when you have to wear
pampers. Fear goes but love lasts. Now there's a line for
Machiavelli's Prince. I learned that from my father. Or is it
the other way around?

Biography

David grew up in Memphis and graduated from U.C.
Berkeley. His poetry can be found in Otoliths (AU), Stony
Thursday Anthology (Ireland), Sentinel Literary Quarterly
(England), and Boxcar Poetry Review (CA), as well as in
publications such as *Poetry Circle*, *FRiGG*, and *The
Offbeat*. His fiction can be read in *Crack the Spine*,
Dodging the Rain, and Every Writer. The Other Is Oneself,
a study of 20th century literature, was published last year in
Germany. He lives in Tokyo.

POETRY

A Charlie Brown Christmas, a poem
https://suddendenouement.com/2017/01/16/a-charlie-brown-christmas-david-lohrey/comment-page-1/#comment-1676

Abomination of Good Cheer, a poem
https://poetrycircle.com/6431/the-abomination-of-good-cheer/

Beneath the Jungle, a poem
http://theoffbeat.submittable.com/user/submissions/6706189

Black and Blue, a poem
http://www.quarterday.org/

Bride in the Sky, a poem
http://ratsassreview.net/?page_id=1070#Lohrey

Captivity, a poem
https://newlondonwriters.com/2017/03/25/captivity/

Chalk Dust and Sand, a poem

https://literaryyard.com/2017/06/01/poem-chalk-dust-and-sand/

Confessions of a Bad Driver, a poem
https://poetrycircle.com/6428/confessions-of-a-bad-driver/
http://friggmagazine.com/issuefortynine/poetry/lohrey/driver.htm

Death Is Not a 5-Star Hotel, a poem
https://newlondonwriters.com/2017/04/01/death-is-not-a-five-star-hotel/

Domestic Violence, a poem
https://outlook.live.com/owa/?id=64855&owa=1&owasuffix=owa%2f&path=/mail/inbox/rp

Drink the Ramen, a poem
http://scars.tv/cgi-bin/framesmain.pl?writers
http://theplumtreetavern.blogspot.jp/search/label/David%20Lohrey
http://www.softblow.org/davidlohrey.html

Eat a Peach, a poem
https://oddballmagazine.com/2017/01/17/13839/
http://www.crackthespine.com/

Evolution of Grief, a poem
http://www.friggmagazine.com/issuefortynine/poetry/lohrey/grief.htm

From the Birds Nest, a poem
http://peekingcatpoetrymagazine.blogspot.jp/p/issues_14.html

Guns and Roses, a poem
https://newpoplitinteractive.wordpress.com/2017/03/28/fun-pop-poetry-28/

Hallelujah Trail, a poem
https://newpoplitinteractive.wordpress.com/2017/01/25/fun-pop-poetry-25/

Hand to Mouth, a poem
http://www.softblow.org/davidlohrey.html

https://boyslutmagazine.com/2017/02/16/david-lohrey/

Holy Smoke, a poem
http://www.friggmagazine.com/issuefortynine/poetry/lohrey/holy.htm

Hudson Canvas, a poem (River View, a poem)
http://www.drunkmonkeys.us/2017-posts/2017/5/12/poetry-hudson-canvas-david-lohrey

Hallelujah Trail, a poem
https://newpoplitinteractive.wordpress.com/tag/david-lohrey/

Humpty Dumpty, a poem
http://abstractmagtv.com/2017/06/29/humpty-dumpty-by-david-lohrey/

Indecent Exposure, a poem
http://www.rebellesociety.com/2017/03/16/davidlohrey-exposure/

Kabuki Lessons, a poem
http://abstractmagtv.com/2017/06/29/kabuki-lessons-by-david-lohrey/

Landscape with Lemonade Stand, a poem
http://sentinelquarterly.com/
https://issuu.com/southernmusepublishers/docs/issue_6

Missing, a poem
https://suddendenouement.com/2016/12/05/finalist-5-of-6-missing-david-lohrey/

Next Door Neighbor, a poem
https://suddendenouement.com/2016/12/13/next-door-neighbor-david-lohrey/

Nightly News, a poem
http://the-otolith.blogspot.jp/2016/11/david-lohrey.html

No Rest for the Wicked, a poem
https://the-otolith.blogspot.jp/2017/06/david-lohrey.html

Outer Space, a poem
https://suddendenouement.com/2016/12/09/outer-space-david-lohrey/

Paradise Is Demanding, a poem
http://scars.tv/cgi-bin/framesmain.pl?writers
http://www.cecileswriters.com/mag/story/paradise-is-demanding/

Stop the Forest Fires, a poem
http://theoffbeat.submittable.com/user/submissions/6706189

Substitute Teaching, a poem
https://poetrycircle.com/?p=6457&preview=1&_ppp=318e149def

The Jungle Beneath, a poem
http://riverfeetpress.submittable.com/user/submissions/6696027

The Rottweiler Next Door, a poem
http://abstractmagtv.com/2017/06/29/the-rottweiler-next-door/

Triumph of the Will, a poem

https://literaryyard.com/2017/06/01/poem-triumph-of-the-will/

61 Is Fine By Me, a poem
http://www.poemsandpoetryblog.com/tag/david-lohrey

CPSIA information can be obtained
at www.ICGtesting.com
Printed in the USA
LVHW021605270319
612036LV00014B/607